Konnichiwa Florida Moon

Konnichiwa Florida Moon

The Story of George Morikami, Pineapple Pioneer

VIRGINIA ARONSON

Pineapple Press, Inc.
Sarasota, Florida

Inquiries should be addressed to:

Pineapple Press, Inc.
P.O. Box 3889
Sarasota, Florida 34230

www.pineapplepress.com

Library of Congress Cataloging-in-Publication Data

Aronson, Virginia.
    Konnichiwa Florida moon : the story of George Morikami, pineapple
pioneer / Virginia Aronson.—1st ed.
        p.   cm.
    Summary: A biography of George Morikami, a Japanese immigrant who
came to south Florida in 1906 and maintained his simple lifestyle even after
becoming a millionaire by acquiring land and growing pineapples.
    Includes bibliographical references.
    ISBN 1-56164-263-0 (alk. paper)
        1. Morikami, George—Juvenile literature. 2. Horticulturists—Florida—
Delray Beach Region—Biography—Juvenile literature. 3. Fruit growers—
Florida—Delray Beach Region—Biography—Juvenile literature. 4. Pineapple—
Florida—Delray Beach Region—Juvenile literature. [1. Morikami, George. 2.
Fruit growers. 3. Japanese Americans—Biography.] I. Title.

SB63.M77 A76 2002
634'.092—dc21
[B]

                                                                    2002025290

First Edition
10 9 8 7 6 5 4 3 2 1

Design by Carol Tornatore
Printed in the United States of America

To my friends in south Florida,
where soft wind still bends coconut palms
in the moonlight.

Konnichiwa Florida Moon

moon (tsuki)

*Broken and broken
again on the sea. the moon
so easily mends.*

—Chosu

As a boy, Sukeji Morikami often watched the glowing moon float gently above the black sea. He lived with his family in Japan, in a fishing hamlet north of the lovely coastal town of Miyazu. He was a good student, bright and hardworking, and his dreams were modest. He loved Japan—the thick swirling mists that followed cool summer rains, the fresh fish he ate raw with a small bowl of rice. His life was simple but rich: the faraway cry of the heron, the dark sky full of the songs of crickets and frogs, his little brother padding behind him on unsteady toddler's legs.

When he reached manhood, Sukeji Morikami honored Japanese custom and approached his girlfriend's parents to ask for her hand in marriage. To his dismay, the Onizawas turned him down. Depressed and confused, the nineteen-year-old stared blindly as the red sun sank low into soft mountains of pink clouds.

Young men from Miyazu were changing their dreams, leaving their homeland for a distant, unknown colony. Sukeji Morikami rashly decided to join them. He quickly signed away the next few years of his life, hiring himself out as an indentured worker. It was the spring of 1906 when "George," who spoke no English and could barely pronounce his American name, shipped out of Miyazu. He was headed for a foundering pineapple-growing operation deep in the wilderness of south Florida.

Young George Morikami

George Morikami's journey to a new life was sponsored by a wealthy silk merchant from Miyazu. Mitsusaburo Oki paid for George's ticket on the *Shinanomaru*, a ship sailing for Seattle, and for the three-thousand-mile train ride to the East Coast of the U.S. In exchange, the poor Japanese boy would spend three years as an unpaid farmhand at the Yamato colony, a new agricultural community on south Florida's Atlantic coast. After that time, George would have fulfilled his debt to his sponsor, and Mr. Oki had promised to pay him a bonus of $500.

Young George Morikami had a new dream. He was determined to return to the land of mountain waterfalls and plum blossoms— with his earnings in hand. He wanted to purchase a hillside plot of fertile Japanese farmland. That way, he was certain he could convince his beloved Hatsue and the rest of the Onizawas he was worthy. He would work hard as the full moon rose and set, rose and set again. Eventually, surely, the Miyazu moon would lie on her back, casting her silvery light on George and his bride.

George's luck, however, did not support this romantic dream. In fact, he never set foot on Japanese soil again. He never saw his true love again either, and Hatsu Onizawa married another suitor. Destiny had other dreams—American dreams—in store for George Morikami.

Bridge of Heaven, Miyazu, Japan, 1915

Florida (Furorida)

Rain went sweeping on
in the twilight, spilling moons
on every grass blade.
—Sho-U

When he arrived in the humid, semitropical jungle that was early south Florida, George's desires were simple. He longed only for a futon, a cotton mattress to lie down and rest upon, and a tiled roof to protect him from the unrelenting sunshine. He wished for *shoji*, sliding paper-covered windows and doors to keep the bloodthirsty mosquitoes at bay. He yearned for steaming cups of green tea, and he imagined relaxing in a *furo*, the traditional Japanese bathing room. He could almost feel the cool mist drifting down from distant snow-capped mountains.

Yamato, the agricultural colony where George had contracted to live and work, was nothing like his hometown in Japan. In fact, Yamato was unique to south Florida in the early 1900s. While the Florida East Coast Railroad had been completed in 1896, stretching from Jacksonville in the north all the way down to Miami at the southern tip of the state, few people were relocating to the vast, unsettled regions in the southernmost parts of Florida. The harsh, overgrown, swampy land was considered unfarmable, the primitive living conditions insufferable. Hurricanes and floods were greatly feared, and air conditioning had yet to be invented. South Florida *was* the Everglades: a buggy, mucky, snake-infested, crocodile-loaded, dangerous no-man's land.

As George rode in a horse-drawn carriage down the sandy trail that served as the main road

Travel by horse-drawn cart in early Florida

into the Yamato colony, black flies buzzed his head and armies of mosquitoes raised dozens of itchy welts. Thick, flat wilderness spread out before him unbroken, neither a hill nor a house in sight. How could anyone possibly hope to grow food crops amid the huge pine and palmetto trees, the endless tangle of razor-sharp sedge appropriately called sawgrass? George watched out carefully for lurking panthers and alligators, water moccasins, and poisonous spiders as big as his fist. He wondered just what he was doing in this strange, isolated, faraway land. Would he ever grow accustomed to the intense glare of the sun, the raw beauty of this primordial marshland called Yamato?

Yamato means "the beginning" in Japanese. The nation of Japan was once called Yamato, too. The word *yamato* had additional, more subtle meanings that the Japanese recognize as aspects of the spirit of the word. To the Japanese, *yamato* once meant "large, peaceful country," and the name denoted happiness, prosperity, good fortune, all the blessings of mankind. *Yamato* spoke of a deep sense of national pride and a feeling of great optimism for the future.

When fewer than a dozen Japanese men first arrived in Wyman in south Florida between 1904 and 1905 to set up a farming community, they held great expectations for their future as Americans. Yamato was the first Japanese colony on the East Coast of the U.S. The Japanese colonists were educated men, political idealists with plans for freedom, democracy, and full

Yamato

assimilation into the American culture. They would prosper on American soil and live out the American dream. The early Yamatoans were humble yet determined—and full of optimism for the ultimate success of their mission.

They were not alone in their adventuresome ideals. A handful of hardy American pioneers had also settled around the Wyman area. Some lived in a little coastal community they called Boca Ratone (later renamed Boca Raton). Others were working small farms a few miles north in Delray Beach.

The American locals quickly welcomed the shy men from Japan, lending a hand to the unskilled laborers. They showed the newcomers the best methods for clearing the rough land, using grubbing hoes, heavy rakes, and shovels. Since they had no tractors, all work was done by hand. Progress was exceedingly slow.

By the time George arrived at Yamato, the group had expanded to more than twenty men. They had cleared a few acres and were living in tents or crude shacks erected to serve as temporary accommodations. Built out of discarded

Early Yamato colony

23

boards from shipwrecks and used packing crates, the houses had no familiar amenities: no futons, shoji, or furo. No tile roofs. No plumbing, little furniture, and not much protection from the oppressive heat and annoying insects. George made himself at home as best he could, resting his weary limbs for the back-breaking labor to come. Even the moon, he noticed, looked different in Florida.

George's American neighbors openly referred to all of the Yamatoans as "Japs." This term is now regarded as an offensive, derogatory name for people of Japanese heritage. Despite the blatant prejudice, the colony was generally accepted into the not-much-greater surrounding community. After all, *everyone* was struggling in the marshy soil, hoping to prosper in south Florida—despite the heavy odds against them.

A newspaper report at the time acknowledged that "the interests of the entire state of Florida are really at heart with the colonists" at Yamato. Indeed, the sparse populace openly supported the efforts of the Japanese colonists. Floridians were hopeful that the colony experiment would succeed, thereby attracting additional settlers, including more foreign laborers. Floridians thought that the Japanese might also develop new crops and inventive agricultural techniques for adoption throughout the state.

George Morikami's shack at Yamato

George, however, felt pessimistic. Lonely and heartsick, he toiled from sunup to sundown, digging in the sand flea–infested soil. His head was encased in bug netting to keep the insects out of his eyes and mouth; his legs were covered by protective canvas to reduce sawgrass wounds. Clearing the land and, later, planting pineapples took up most of George's time and all of his energy. The summer heat never let up; cool winds failed to arrive. He was always exhausted, and he

George Morikami and Yamato colonists, 1906

could not shake the feeling of deep isolation as his ignorance of the American language and culture continued unchanged. The unfamiliar Florida moon waxed and waned at a distance.

"I came here in 1906," George told a Miami newspaper reporter in one of his few interviews, given the year he died. "I was the only one of my people who was uneducated. They were all educated. I couldn't speak or write English." In reality, George *was* educated—in Japanese. He

had attended the lower and higher elementary schools in Miyazu, graduating at age fourteen. But the other young men who had colonized Yamato were fluent in English. Some were college educated, and several had American schooling. George felt like an outcast, an outsider in an alien community in an isolated outpost in no-man's land in a foreign country! No wonder the yellow moon seemed so far away, reckless rain splashing on rain in the airless damp of the tropical night.

"I just wanted to save a little money and

George Morikami and colonists in pineapple field, 1906

go back home," George admitted in the Miami interview. "But at the end of three years, I looked and I had no money. Not even enough to go back home on. So I had to stay here."

George's luck had not improved. After six hard months of hot, sweaty, unpaid labor at Yamato, he was suddenly left without a sponsor when Mr. Oki fell ill and died. Epidemics were all too common in early Florida, frequent floods carrying diseases like malaria and typhoid. Colonists who succumbed were cremated, their ashes returned to Japan. George stayed healthy, but after his three-year stint was completed he was flatly informed that he would never receive his $500 bonus payment.

Not surprisingly, George decided to abandon the still-struggling Japanese farm colony. He desperately wanted to learn the English language, and he was intent on familiarizing himself with American culture. George's newest dream was to prosper on his own in the country he could not afford to leave.

Yamato schoolhouse, class of 1921–1922

He found himself a job in a coastal town some 120 miles to the north. After boarding with and laboring long hours for an American ship-building family in Eau Gallie (now part of Melbourne), George moved in with the Ohi family. Also from Miyazu, the Ohis operated a small farm worked by family members and other Japanese immigrants. Mr. Ohi had left the Yamato colony the same year George had joined it. Mr. Ohi was fluent in English and had quickly become a successful farmer.

It was 1910 and George was almost twenty-four years old. With the encouragement of the Ohis, he enrolled in the Eau Gallie public school—grade 5. Understandably, George felt out of step with his young classmates. But he spent the school year studying diligently, becoming fluent in the language and some of the customs of his adopted homeland.

In the meantime, the Yamato colony thrived, peaked, and dwindled—several times. Floods, blights, and changing markets destroyed the

pineapple (pinappuru)

budding pineapple business, which was replaced by citrus trees, tomato crops, and other successful winter vegetables. Wives arrived from Japan, children were born, and a post office and a public school were built. The colonists wore slippers around their comfortable, sparsely furnished homes, where they ate their rice with chopsticks. But they shot pool, too, and indulged in hand-cranked ice cream, and only the adults spoke Japanese anymore.

When George returned to the Yamato area in 1912, a friend living in Delray Beach offered him the opportunity to farm half an acre. Despite the torrential rains, ongoing attacks by hungry worms and grasshoppers, and a lack of funds for supplies, George was able to harvest eighty-four bushels of tomatoes that year. At the end of his first full season as an independent farmer, George had a bumper crop—and he'd earned $1,000 in profits. His luck was changing, but very, very slowly.

garden (niwa)

Since my house burned down.
I now own a better view
of the rising moon.
—Masahide

*B*etween World Wars I and II, George gradually enlarged his farm and developed a busy mail-order business for marketing south Florida produce. When the banks failed in 1929 and the Great Depression impoverished the country, all of George's savings were lost. But he held on to his land.

By the time World War II was under way, only a few families remained at Yamato. Former Yamatoans had assimilated into the surrounding communities; others had moved or returned to Japan. In 1942, the colony's land was confiscated by the American government. The U.S. Army was building a five-thousand-acre military airfield and radar training school in Boca Raton. Sadly, the U.S. Army Air Corps Technical Training Station purposely destroyed all of the buildings on the Yamato property during target practice. U.S. Army trainees jokingly—and crudely—referred to Yamato as "Blitz Village."

George's land remained his own. But times were exceedingly tough, and the Japanese living in America were regarded with anger and suspicion. Unlike Japanese Americans who resided in California during the war, Floridians of Japanese descent were not relocated to internment camps. But they were carefully watched and rigidly restricted in their activities and travel. Japanese Americans living in Florida were questioned by the FBI. Their homes were searched and they were told not to leave their counties. They even needed special permission to withdraw money from their own bank accounts! Prejudice was rampant and often cruel.

George's produce marketing business was seized by the U.S. government five days after Japan bombed Pearl Harbor. A twenty-four-hour guard was assigned by the U.S. Coast Guard to monitor George's daily life. In Delray Beach, he was scorned by former friends. Merchants refused to sell him the seeds and fertilizer he needed to continue farming his land.

George's farm was suffering too. As he recalled for a news reporter some thirty years later, "I was hardly making things go. Then a storm came and washed out my crop." He approached a local bank for help. "When I was dead broke and I needed the money, the bank wouldn't lend it to me," George remembered sadly. He was, after all, from Japan—despite his nearly forty years spent farming American soil.

As was his habit, George remained steadfast and continued to work the fickle Florida land, doing his best with what he had. The cicadas buzzed in the scrub pine; the sickle moon sliced through the night sky. Snail kites swooped; huge turkey vultures banked in the breeze. George cleared the sawgrass from the land and dug in the sandy soil. When his harvests succeeded, George used his profits to purchase additional acreage. "I bought the land at fifteen dollars an acre. Some I bought at seventeen dollars an acre. . . . In those days, you put down as much money as you could and you pay the rest when you can," George later explained.

In this way, George eventually amassed more than 150 acres of south Florida land. With the invention of air conditioning, the area was becoming increasingly popular as a destination for vacationers and retirees. As highways and con-dominiums spread into sprawl, the value of George's property climbed steadily. He continued to buy up acres of undeveloped land.

By 1967, George could count twenty thou-sand pineapple plants flowering in his fields, and he patiently continued to expand his harvest.

That same year, he became an official U.S. citizen. "I never really thought it would ever happen," he told a friend after being sworn in on December 15. Despite the biased treatment he had received, especially during World War II, George loved America and was proud to be an American.

On January 2, 1968, the city of Delray Beach appointed George Morikami as honorary mayor. By that time, the value of his land—much of it located in Delray—had soared to more than $10,000 an acre. The honorary mayor was a millionaire. His luck had truly changed.

George continued to farm the land, making his home in an old yellow trailer nestled in his fields. A hired crew had dug a large lake on his property, and in this burst of blue water George bathed, swam, and fished. A floating feeder for ducks bobbed gently in the middle of the clear, cool lake.

George kept a mound of the excavated dirt directly across the lake from his four-room mobile home. Before sunrise, he could stand silently in

George Morikami's pineapple crop, 1965

hello (konnichiwa)

George Morikami and a perfect pineapple, 1966

Florida pineapples, 1920s

George Morikami at age 82

front of his house, watching the mist creep over the dirt hill he referred to as his own "Little Mount Fuji" (named after the largest volcano in Japan). Peace and contentment settled over him at night when the fat moon filled up the sky.

Always a private person, George led a quiet life alone on his farm. A lifelong bachelor, he enjoyed reading and tending to his crops. His garden contained more than forty varieties of plants and trees. He ate the food he grew himself: pineapples, small white peaches, blackberries, persimmons and papayas, squash, cucumbers, peppers, tomatoes, beans, sweet onions, and white radishes. Consulting back issues of *Organic Gardening* magazine, George regularly experimented with unusual crops. One time, a friend brought back papaya seeds from Hawaii. George devised ingenious methods for protecting the trees from fruit flies, including an intricate latticework fence wrapped with mosquito netting.

Patient as the stars and in sync with nature, George ate, slept, and worked according to an inner time clock. He rose with the sun, made simple uncooked meals whenever he wished, and napped in his fields under the shade of the mango trees. He bounced about his property in an ancient tractor, using the headlights to perform midnight farming efforts.

"I like this," he explained one day when he was eighty-nine years old, gnarled and shuffling, dressed in tattered clothing. "It is simple. The land is all around me. I eat fresh fruits and vegetables I grow myself. No meat. I eat when I am hungry, day or night. If I had to live in town, I couldn't have this. . . The land is not for sale at any price." Neither was the dream of self-sufficiency, labor rewarded by prosperity, and his own plot of rich earth.

Despite lucrative offers from the developers who were tearing up south Florida, George refused to sell off any of his land. In 1975, he donated forty acres to the University of Florida for use as an experimental farm. Later, he gave over one hundred acres to the Palm Beach Department of Parks and Recreation, hanging on to his lake and the surrounding farmland he still tended. In his will, the remainder of his property was left to the county to be used for a public park.

When George Morikami died on February 29, 1976, he was the last surviving Yamato colonist—and he was still growing pineapples! The two-hundred-acre park that would bear his name was under construction. An architect's design for a museum that George had requested for the park hung above the couch where he slept on the last night of his long life.

A little over a year later, the Morikami Museum and Park was opened to the public. In 2001, with the construction of one of the largest Japanese gardens in the U.S., the land where George once harvested his pineapples became known as the Morikami Museum and Japanese Gardens. The park is a lush oasis of natural beauty in the midst of overdeveloped south Florida. A simple Japanese-style headstone marks the quiet place in the park where George's ashes are buried.

simple life, or life itself (issei)

Behind me the moon
brushes a shadow of pines
lightly on the floor.
—Kikaku

Georege Morikami was a penniless immigrant when he first set foot on Florida marshland. The sandy, tangled, often-flooded, always bug-infested land eventually transformed him into a millionaire. But this miraculous turn of events did not occur over-night—nor did it change the soul of the man.

Sukeji Morikami lived a simple life on his plot of Florida land. For seventy years, he faith-fully tilled the earth. He watched the full moon rise, over and over again, lighting gently the tangle of sawgrass before him. In his daily efforts, he displayed a deep respect for nature as he honored both his traditional homeland and the country where he lived the bulk of his life. He bowed to the earth, a small bent form at the dip of the Florida sky.

With decades of humility and unceasing labor, George Sukeji Morikami fulfilled the American dream of rags-to-riches success. His legacy includes the preservation of his valuable land, along with his inspirational example. Perhaps we, too, will learn to bow to the earth— no matter where we are born, no matter where we spend our lives. For it is the land, George Morikami believed, that gives us all life.

Author's Note
and Acknowledgments

George Morikami was a private person who shared little of his personal life with others. I have taken poetic liberties with his story to convey what I imagined were some of his feelings and emotions as he struggled to survive—and prosper—in an inhospitable land.

The poetry included throughout the story is haiku, a traditional Japanese literary form. In each three-lined poem, nature's beauty and a sense of season are conveyed within brief phrasing. Haiku is as simple and lovely as a Japanese garden.

The employees of the Morikami Museum and Japanese Gardens were helpful to me when I was researching this book. Peg McCall at the Boca Raton Historical Society provided me with as much archival material as she could find. Virginia Snyder, a close friend of George Morikami, reviewed the manuscript and pointed out errors. Any mistakes in the content of this book are my own.

Japanese symbols (*shuuji*) by Hayato Imai and Norimasa Kariya. Photos courtesy of the Florida State Archives.

Japanese symbols
(shuuji)

hello (konnichiwa)

moon (tsuki)

Florida (Furorida)

Yamato

pineapple (pinappuru)

garden (niwa)

simple life, or life itself (issei)

Bibliography

Behn, Harry, trans. *Cricket Songs: Japanese Haiku.* New York: Harcourt, Brace and World, 1964.

Boca Raton Historical Society. *The Spanish River Papers* (Spring 1985), Vol. 13, No. 3.

Boca Raton Historical Society. *The Spanish River Papers* (October 1977), Vol. 6, No 1.

Fernald, Edward A., ed. *Atlas of Florida.* Gainesville, FL: University Press of Florida, 1992.

Gannon, Michael, ed. *The New History of Florida.* Gainesville, FL: University Press of Florida, 1996.

Lloyd, Joanne M. "'Yankees of the Orient': Yamato and Japanese Immigration to America" (masters thesis). Florida Atlantic University, 1990.

Scarangello, Dominick J. "The Yamato Colony and the Japanese Colonization Movement to the Eastern United States" (masters thesis). Florida State University, 1996.

Snyder, Virginia. "Sole Survivor," *Palm Beach Life* (May 1993).

The Morikami Museum and Japanese Gardens

The Morikami Museum and Japanese Gardens is located at 4000 Morikami Park Road in Delray Beach, Florida. The museum preserves and interprets Japanese culture as part of Florida history and features exhibits of traditional and modern Japanese art and culture, including a traditional Japanese home that visitors tour wearing paper slippers. Seasonal festivals, tea ceremonies, and such traditional crafts as origami and kite-making are offered to visitors. The gardens and two-hundred-acre park evoke a distinctive Oriental character with fish ponds, waterfalls, arched bridges, and bonsai displays.

The museum offers school tour programs that feature permanent and changing exhibits. Pre- and post-visit activities further enrich students' explorations of Japan and of Florida history. Teachers' packets, developed by the Morikami Education Department, are also available to help educators introduce information on Japanese cultural traditions into their classrooms. Visit the museum's website at www.morikami.org for more information on activities, tours, and teachers' packets.

About the Author

VIRGINIA ARONSON has written more than two dozen published books. About half of these titles are for young readers, including biographies of tennis stars Venus and Serena Williams and of the founder of Motown Records, Berry Gordy. She lives with her writer husband and young son in Boca Raton, Florida, a few miles from the land once owned by the Yamato colony. Her family's garden includes tomatoes, corn, squash, strawberries, citrus, bananas, and mangoes—but, alas, no pineapples.

If you enjoyed reading this book, here are some other books from Pineapple Press on related topics. Ask your local bookseller for our books. For a complete catalog, write to Pineapple Press, P.O. Box 3889, Sarasota, FL 34230 or call 1-800-PINEAPL (746-3275). Or visit our website at www.pineapplepress.com.

Gift of the Unicorn: The Story of Lue Gim Gong, Florida's Citrus Wizard by Virginia Aronson. Lue Gim Gong left his native China and sailed to the United States in 1872 at the age of 12. Thus began his lifelong journey of discovery and experimentation with several different crops that would finally win him the grudging admiration of his fellow Americans. Illustrated with archive photos, this book, part of the Pineapple Press Biographies for Young Readers series, is perfect for children aged 9–12. ISBN 1-56164-264-9 (hb)

Dinosaurs of the South by Judy Cutchins and Ginny Johnston. This third volume in the Southern Fossil Discoveries series offers new and exciting information to reveal the lives of dinosaurs in the Southern coastal states. Like its companion volumes, *Ice Age Giants of the South* and *Giant Predators of the Ancient Seas,* this book is rich with dozens of color photos and original art. ISBN 1-56164-266-5 (hb)

The Florida Water Story by Peggy Sias Lantz and Wendy A. Hale. Illustrates and describes many of the plants and animals that depend on the springs, rivers, beaches, marshes, and reefs in and around Florida, including corals, sharks, lobsters, alligators, manatees, birds, and turtles. ISBN 1-56164-099-9 (hb)

Giant Predators of the Ancient Seas by Judy Cutchins and Ginny Johnston. Second in the Southern Fossil Discoveries series, this companion to *Ice Age Giants of the South* explores how scientists use fossil clues to learn about the lives and habitats of the most exciting sea animals that ever lived. ISBN 1-56164-237-1 (hb)

Ice Age Giants of the South by Judy Cutchins and Ginny Johnston. First in the Southern Fossil Discoveries series, this book chronicles up-to-date discoveries in the field of archaeology and describes how prehistoric animals looked, how they lived, and what they ate. Includes full-color photos of fossil bones, reconstructed skeletons, and lifelike models of extinct creatures. ISBN 1-56164-195-2 (hb)

The Young Naturalist's Guide to Florida by Peggy Sias Lantz and Wendy A. Hale. Plants, birds, insects, reptiles, and mammals are all around us. This enticing book shows you where and how to look for Florida's most interesting natural features and creatures. ISBN 1-56164-051-4 (pb)